Advance Praise for HUMAN VOICES WAKE US

"Jerald Winakur's *Human Voices Wake Us* carries the reader into that deep place where poetry and medicine intersect and generate healing. His poems celebrate beauty in the natural world, not in abstract terms but in its particularity, in bluegills, dragonflies, dust devils, and prickly pear. They celebrate the wisdom of story, as when a student asks him, 'Are butterflies birds?' Or when he tells the story of Mick and the hamburger. And they celebrate the practice of medicine in all its sorrows and joys, but especially compassionate solidarity with patients. In 'This Sadness,' a poem about cancer, Dr. Winakur writes, 'this sadness / does not speak the language.' But this poet-physician *does* speak the language, the language of healing through poetry. A marvelous collection!"
　—JACK COULEHAN, author of *The Wound Dresser*

"Jerald Winakur's *Human Voices Wake Us* is more than a collection of exquisitely crafted poems. There is such poignancy here, such humility, such a keen, painful awareness of the fleetingness of our little lives, of the agonizing drifts and decisions facing us as we age, that it is impossible to put this book down. Winakur's poems are wide open to anguish and joy—especially the small but intense joys we can find in great blue herons, forsythia, dogwoods, redbuds, owlet moths, wheatgrass, little bluestem, tall fescue, and maidencane. As he says in 'A Denunciation of Quarks,' 'I am no longer certain what matters, want / only to touch the thing itself for once.' And touch the things of this living world Winakur does, with vividness and care, even as we mourn the limitations of our little lives. 'I have done the best I could,' laments Winakur in 'Out of Practice,' and these poems certainly convince us that before retiring as a physician, Winakur did more than his best. If only we could have been fortunate enough to have been one of his patients. But how lucky we are to have these poems that, even as they mourn the limitations of the best medical practices and the often humiliating and agonizing realities of our aging, offer us medical advice for all our lives, to live wide awake to the sensory joys that continually surround us."
　—WENDY BARKER, author of *One Blackbird at a Time*

HUMAN VOICES WAKE US

Human Voices Wake Us

Poems by

JERALD WINAKUR

◞

THE KENT STATE UNIVERSITY PRESS

Kent, Ohio

Library of Congress Catalog Number 2016055041
ISBN 978-1-60635-334-9
Manufactured in the United States of America

LIBRARY OF CONGRESS CATALOGING-IN-PUBLICATION DATA
Names: Winakur, Jerald, author.
Title: Human voices wake us / Poems by Jerald Winakur.
Description: Kent, Ohio : The Kent State University Press, [2017] | Series: Literature
     and medicine
Identifiers: LCCN 2016055041 (print) | LCCN 2017007337 (ebook) | ISBN
     9781606353349 (pbk. : alk. paper) | ISBN 9781631012907 (ePub) | ISBN
     9781631012914 (ePDF)
Subjects: LCSH: Physician and patient. | Medicine and art. | Poetry.
Classification: LCC R727.3 .W56 2017 (print) | LCC R727.3 (ebook) | DDC
     610.7306/99--dc23
LC record available at https://lccn.loc.gov/2016055041

21 20 19 18 17   5 4 3 2 1

FOR MY DAUGHTERS

and, of course, for

LEE

Contents

Foreword

On *Human Voices Wake Us*

ALAN SHAPIRO

On every page of Jerald Winakur's *Human Voices Wake Us* we are reminded of the kinship between art and medicine, poetry and healing, how care for the vulnerable and mortal body isn't merely rational or scientific, but a supreme act of imagination. The love, insight, and sensitivity embodied in this humane and beautiful book demonstrate how at their best both medicine and poetry (and art in general) engage a combination of faculties we normally think of as antithetical, but in the hands of such an accomplished poet (or healer) become different facets of a single act of attention. The ideal doctor is capable of both appreciating beauty and analyzing symptoms, of empathic devotion and professional distance in the same way that a poet at his or her best must exercise both sympathetic understanding and intellectual clarity in translating pain and suffering into language whose beauty refuses to simplify or ignore what it can't redeem or transcend.

The poems in this book are unflinchingly direct, plainspoken, and elegant. They confront and embrace the inescapable realities of human vulnerability, attachment, loss, and time; they acknowledge the limits of care even while they celebrate the irreplaceable value of care. The book reads like a novel in verse. And yet the poems themselves are individually strikingly distinct. Many are unadorned poems of direct statement that employ a minimum of figuration and punctuation, and thereby generate a noticeably unnoticeable beauty:

THIS SADNESS

> is a cancer
>> for which there is no cure
>>> a surgeon might
>
> cut it out from its roots
>> but it would grow back
>>> an obstetrician might attempt

a high forceps delivery
    a psychiatrist might try to talk it out
        but this sadness

        does not speak the language.

There are poems like "Plastic Caskets" that satirize with great wit the business of death that preys on anxiety and fear:

Anticipating the boom in the demise of Boomers
they're fashioning terminal boxes out of space-age
material selling them mail-order through Amazon.
The same stuff as your hula hoop and Tonka toys
like the bumpers on your BMW like the tiles
on the Shuttle for God's sake . . .

In "What We Said," we find a rueful unforgettable prose poem that's part narrative, part mini-play about the discrepancy between what the doctor wants to say to a terminal patient desperate to be cured, and what his profession obliges him to say:

Here is what I wanted to say: Go home. Get out of this place. Eat chocolate and pizza, ice cream and French fries when you can, go fishing, take a trip around the world, tell your kids you love them, read mystery novels, go to the movies, watch the clouds drift by, write your memoir, make love to your wife. But go just go.

I guess I should fight this thing right doc? he said.

You should I said.

And then there are stunning pastoral poems in this book, like "Gardeners," another form of healing, or "Redbud," an exquisite lyric celebration of persistence and beauty in a mutable death-haunted world:

March—I walk
the ravines, the treed
windbreaks, the creek bottom
all the wooded places

searching for redbuds.
One hundred acres and you

are the only one I have ever found
and I never know

waiting through each winter
if you have survived—
your spindly trunk
born from the side of dead oak

and year after year
you bend more and more
toward the light which filters
through the canopy

of hackberry and cedar.
In one night a winter-hungry deer
might strip your bark
down through the cambium

and you'd be gone.
But this morning here you are
your blossoms fragile, so few
the color so faint it's fanciful

to call it red.
Here you are
and here I am
hanging on.

From poem to poem, Winakur engages passion and cool judgment, sense and intellect; he combines empathy and critical awareness, the long metaphysical view and the up close and personal perspective. He is painfully aware of the limits of medicine, but that awareness only deepens his devotion to the healing arts. That commitment to what he recognizes as inadequate though necessary is a measure of this poet-doctor's humane and inclusive vision of what it means to be alive. *Human Voices Wake Us* should be required reading not just for every medical student or health care professional, but for anyone (meaning all of us) giving or receiving care, having to live, love, and celebrate under the shadow of death.

ALAN SHAPIRO
William R. Kenan Jr. Distinguished Professor of English and Creative Writing
University of North Carolina—Chapel Hill

Introduction

My high school homeroom class counted the last seconds out loud together before the final bell each morning. They waited to see if I might make it before Mr. Martin closed the door; or if he, once again, would be forced to reach for his pad of tardy forms and send me to the principal's office.

If I scuttled through on time the class applauded and I blushed. I have always had a problem with blushing. Mr. Martin, who was also our English teacher, soon stopped sending me to the principal if I was late. I realize now that he watched my approach from his desk, through the window that overlooked the half-deserted school yard. I have no doubt that he saw me there, dawdling after all the others came in. Saw me watching the cardinals call from the tops of the stately oaks, or the eastern towhees forage under the hedges. Or just sitting on the steps watching the last yellow forsythia blooms drop to the ground.

Which is perhaps why, when it was the time of year to engage our class in the "Poetry Unit," he did something unusual. Something else that made me blush. He called on me to read "The Love Song of J. Alfred Prufrock" out loud to the class just at the end of the period. I knew nothing of poetry then, its power to distill and intensify our own inner voices. Even now I recall the emotions—shorn from conscious understanding—that welled up in me as I read. How my voice caught at times; my face flushed; how I never heard the bell ring; how I sat at my desk for a long moment after everyone had filed out of the room. And how, in some vital way, I have never been the same.

At the end of senior year my grandmother died a yellowing death from pancreatic cancer. Since her home was a refuge from my own, on many occasions I was with her when her kind geriatrician visited, sat by her side, held her hand, and injected her with morphine. Once, near the end, she looked up at me and said, "One day you will help people just like he does." Somehow she knew what I then did not.

In college, I was a biology major. *Bios.* Life. I loved the natural world, studied ecology. Every new bird I identified became my favorite. But in pre-med, there was no time for poetry. No time—it seemed to me then—to look differently at the world; to see the thing only for itself. There were just the sciences of deconstruction, smaller and smaller parts: anatomy, physiology, organic chemistry, physics. There was no one in those days who asked: *But what about your inner life? Who will nurture your empathy? What is there once the formulas and theorems are forgotten?*

And suddenly medical school. Like generations of students before me—and since—I was formulated, pinned. Mind-numbing memorization. Fear of failure. I was open to patients and their stories; they wanted, needed my attention. I was in awe of their human voices. But science reigned, not anecdote. One mentor asked: *How many times can you treat someone with heart failure before you get bored by it?* For two stultifying summers I found myself in some research lab learning how to turn living tissue into mitochondria.

Then one of my classmates killed himself. Was it worth it, after all?

I rebelled against the rote-mongers. They almost kicked me out. But then I fell in love with a fellow student and that saved me. Love always does. That and reading, though nothing approved of in that pre–medical humanities era.

I was saved until I learned enough so that I could be of some use to my patients, until the work could save me. By listening to their voices, being attentive to their stories, I could help them. Sometimes I could cure them. And if I could not, they needed my presence, my comforting words, my slowly accreting wisdom. I practiced beneficence; they respected me. There was a kind of mutual love, risky to reveal in this hypersensitive age. In the end, I was glad to be of use.

Almost four decades passed as I scuttled from office to ER to hospital to ICU to nursing home and back and forth and back and forth. My children grew up and left home; I did not nurture my love nor myself. I no longer heard the singing; I was drowning in the midst of a full life. Eventually my patients—so trusting, so stalwart in the face of what we will all face—died no matter what I did or did not do. My father developed Alzheimer's disease. Before he passed he no longer knew my name. And I was afraid.

And yet I put one foot in front of the other, day after day, year after year. I never missed work, or a patient on rounds who needed to be seen. I never yelled at a nurse, threw an instrument across the room, drank more than three beers a year, used an illicit substance, or attempted suicide. And still I was afraid.

Afraid of making a mistake, missing a diagnosis; of injuring or killing someone in my charge. Hundreds of decisions were mine to make every day. How many could I possibly get right? Or dropping a page, or not hearing the phone ring in the night. My hair was growing thin. Each morning I put on my doctor face; I had no time in the day for myself, for lunch, not even a peach.

For me, coming and going in the rooms on daily rounds was not enough to sustain a full life. I believe many of us in medicine feel this way.

I started to write. Many doctors write. The brilliant ones—W. C. Williams comes to mind—enhanced and advanced the canon; helped us see and hear in a different way. I had no such aspirations; there was no moment of my greatness.

Not that I didn't work hard at the poetry. I took creative writing seminars at night and the occasional weekend; and then a rare summer workshop week away, to study with some master, to be critiqued, judged. To be alone, to weep, to pray, to make space for a hundred visions and revisions. To get away from the dyings. Even if my metaphors are mixed, I thought, no one will die.

Most doctors who write poetry, I suspect, write for the same reasons anyone does. To try to capture fleeting thoughts or arresting images; to be enthralled by words and their sounds; to make sense out of hard reality; to converse with oneself and perhaps even others. To overcome frustration, fear. To do intellectual and artistic battle with demons. To mourn, to praise, to remember, to love. To feel alive in the face of a certain doom. To find a way to overcome all that afflicts us.

I am retired now. I have more time to read, to reflect, to write, to teach. There is love in my life once more. Lark sparrows and bobwhites forage among the native grasses I have replanted; turkeys at the feeder morning and evening, wood ducks on the pond. Once more there is singing. Even though I am closer to the end than I have ever been, there is singing.

Doctors these days are struggling so. Debt, divorce, drug addiction, alcoholism, suicide. They succeed or fail on professional treadmills; patient encounters are measured out with coffee spoons. The doctor-patient relationship is crumbling. Bureaucratic and corporate masters oversee, make their never-ending arguments of insidious intent. And financial recompense, for most called to minister, has never been the "force that through the green fuse drives the flower."

The overwhelming questions: Now where to turn? How do we avoid being crushed by the demands of Science, of Perfection, of Expectations? How do we recover the awe we once felt in this world in which we expend our life force every day? How can we find joy in the thing itself once more?

For me it is this: Reflect each day on the patients you care for. Be attentive to those who are struggling with illness, with age, with infirmity, with loss. Hear their human voices; recognize how noble they are in the battles they fight and how important is your role as healer and advocate. See the world through their eyes and do your best day in and day out to help them negotiate the medical morass you know awaits them. Nurture that idealism, that empathic responsiveness that first brought you into medicine long ago. Be glad to be of use.

This is what I try to impart to my students, the ones who find their way into the "Medicine Through Literature" class I co-teach with my poet-novelist-lawyer wife, Lee Robinson. This class is a small part of an educational renaissance, the medical humanities movement.

Each September when I see the young, often worried, reticent, sometimes anxious faces of our students file into our seminar room—after they have spent so long lingering in the chambers of universities and hospital wards—I am so hopeful. I say that we want them to bring their whole selves to this class; that they do not have to fear the feelings they may have buried during that ER Trauma rotation, that time in the neonatal ICU, those daily losses on the geriatric ward. Or that time they, out of fear of retribution, kept silent as one of their own was berated or harassed by someone with power. Tell us these stories, reveal these feelings. Do not dissociate from these events.

I want to help them nurture themselves and their patients-to-be with the readings we have chosen for the year. Stories and essays and poems by the masters, by other health care professionals, and by patients themselves. About the human condition, about crisis and loss; about how to keep from drowning. I want them to know with all certainty that these voices—and their own—can enrich and enhance their lifetime in medicine.

I want the works we explore together to serve as bulwarks against their own trials and losses which are coming—whether they know it or not yet in their young lives. They must proceed fearlessly against the infirmities of their patients—and then against their own.

And while the ethicists preach that autonomy is modern medicine's guiding principle, I demur. It is beneficence by which we will be redeemed. It is love that swells the singing only you can hear.

I want to take these future patients by the hand—each to each—and say, *Let us go then, you and I . . .*

First Do No Harm

This is the main thing
they preach

as you make your
way to the steel table

where she awaits
you

and that first
bloodless slice.

What harm can you do here?
Then all the doing comes

all the sleepless nights
until one day blood blooms

as you draw the blade
through live flesh

where anything and everything
can go wrong

and it will
it does.

Look: you are the one
wielding the steel

above your own
head

so much cutting
so much falls away

so much
left behind.

First do
no harm.

And all this time
you thought

they were talking about
someone else.

The Emu in the Graveyard

Neither one of us belongs.
Me—my grandma Bessie's golden boy—
here on this limestone rise above the Guadalupe
in cowboy hat and bolo tie.
Him—goose-stepping among the stones
over these long-dead German settlers:
Freidenker they called themselves—Freethinkers

Now all of that is out of favor:
their atheism, his not-white-enough meat.
And what is a single emu when it comes
to a pair of boots? Maybe enough for a single
sole—like mine—alone today and reading the old tablets:
this one died in childbirth, that one of the grippe
all these babies gone before penicillin

not one older than I am now—freethinker
who won't betray his reckoning.
The emu never comes at you straight on:
he sidles among the stones, disappears
in the shadows of the moss-choked oaks
tiny brain bobbing on that sidewinder neck.
Those unblinking prehistoric wall-eyes

throw only a sideways glance
that will never let me forget.

Vigil, 1958

I was born into this world too soon, too frail
to be saved by Darwin's rationale of tooth
and claw: that the fastest gazelle is sure proof
the stalking lion won't always prevail.
I guess it made a kind of sense, fast genes
rewarded so the predator in turn
must do better yet in order to earn
her place in the copulatory scheme.
A boy, I bred guppies, kept the vigil
as a gravid female dropped child after
silver-flecked child into the crowded waters
of her own birth and life and death, that bowl
my cosmos. I turn away, unwilling
to witness mothers devour their young.

Forest Hills Park, Spring 1994

I have returned, opened myself again
like the dogwood the forsythia
to this unchanging cityscape where

time passes in pigeon-steps
and too many seasons separate me from Lena
my grandma Bessie's sister, a last

flickering link. She always apologizes:
I don't know why Bessie was taken so young
and I am still here. I fumble once more for a reply.

Then as always I say: As long as you
are here she is here. Lena shakes
her head slows her walk leans more into me.

She is so frail now; this will be the last visit.
And then I understand. Finally
I turn to her and say: I love you.

And I still need you here.
We sit on the bench shielding each other
from the wind watching the dogwoods bloom

white as the sheets on my grandmother's bed
the forsythia yellow as her skin
the day she died and Lena held me tight.

Pawn Shop Dreams

For almost forty years
my father doesn't sleep
remembering that night
in America

no one in Baltimore slept
while the looting the burning
swept the city ending
his life's work

in another Kristallnacht.
Nightmares of Cossacks
shook his father awake
and now my father dreams

of men ripping off iron grates
smashing windows torching showcases
burrowing through the roof running off
with watches and radios pledged by others

coming at him at him at him.
He told me after: *it's best this way*
now you won't be hostage to that shop
you must be somebody. . . .

And I tried: the white coat, the Oath
the secondhand dream the years
of practice practice practice
those calls in the night: blue newborns

feverish infants, smokers suffocating
alcoholics puking blood, young men
crushed by chest pain
strangled by cancers

old men babbling, wasting away.
My father still doesn't sleep
and now neither do I: pledged neurons
dying even as I dream.

Are Butterflies Birds?

—for MLR

I was the larval lab instructor when she asked me that.
She a freshman who smelled not yet of formaldehyde
but of honey, with dark bee eyes in which I saw myself
refracted, as if viewed from every angle.

A giant owlet moth pinned to paraffin before her, wings
of feathery silk spread wider than any sparrow's—
her question seems so natural now.
But then I laughed, lectured on bugs and backbones

a chrysalis of taxonomy in which I lay enmeshed, arrested
at some early stage, clinging to some familiar limb.
She listened, smiled, and moved her eyes from mine
searching for someone less camouflaged.

And she may have been the one.
Too long entombed, I have awakened to the thrum
of hummingbirds, tickled by tongues seeking nectar
to the blue flash of buntings in the brush

to the soaring, circling raptors drawing me into their vortex
to the kamikaze plunges of pelicans on the brink of extinction
to the black and orange mass of monarchs floating
migrating to misted mountain valleys.

Now I would answer her: *Yes.* Of course butterflies are birds.
I can imagine us, imagoes, drifting on cool currents
of rarefied air, coming to rest face to face, wings
folded back, resembling the leaves from which we arose.

Taos, 4 July, 2100 Hours

It rained hard all afternoon
this being the rainy season
the field was a sea of mud
me in my white Explorer
him in his banged-up '69 Chevy,
paintless

we sat waiting for the fireworks
he got out to watch
his son light a bottle rocket
a kid the same age as mine
not quite grown. . . .
A father's reflex

he moved him away
from the flame-spewing thing
cigarette dangling from his lips
chugging Bud after Bud
black braid whipping his
tattooed shoulders

and I wondered
what are we—he and I—doing here
me high on the trout streams
him holiday drunk
the drowned field was filling up with cars
sky darkening

the peaks a purple
mountain majesty when he got
out again to take a wavering piss
I reclined in my bucket seat
the first rockets tore into the sky
bursting just

above our heads
white-hot streaks slashing
through the night
red white and blue flame
cascading down on us
the eerie whistling

of the steaming gases the streaked heavens
the bone-jarring thunder of exploding ordnance
echoed through the mountains
through the years
and a familiar light illuminated
that muddy paddy

and us
then he screamed: INCOMING!
dove trembling back into his car
and more than a few people laughed
but he didn't
and neither did I.

A Denunciation of Quarks

This disconnect between the subatomic world and the world of humans is good for the soul. It shows us that our day-to-day perceptions do not apply to every facet of existence.
—Newsweek, *May 9, 1994*

I have spent my life deconstructing in search of quarks
those tiniest of subatomic particles absent
from the Universe since the Big Bang
eons before, and lasting only a hundred billionth
of a trillionth of a second—if at all extant.

As minute bits of mass hurtled through the dark
smashing together like frightened subway strangers
I peered at fleeting phosphorescent products of decay
never sure what was real, what was artifact
unconvinced by any single event.

Now I fear there will be no exaltation of larks
that I will never even hear one deep in the brush.
I am no longer certain what matters, want
only to touch the thing itself for once. Unless I bump
into you again there will be no Eureka moment.

How long must something exist—no matter how stark—
before it is real enough for the final ascent?

Blown Pupil

When they pulled back your lids in the ICU
the right pupil was liquid, black
much bigger than the left
which remained pinpoint
the hemorrhage having

paralyzed the nerve in your innocent eye
a blown pupil they said
the respirator hissing and clicking
next to your bed.
Old friend

when they turned off the machine
I watched your chest settle
for the last time
closed your lids and then
the corneas covering them both

went for salvage, a good thing
I guess.
That I'm still here
seems lopsided
like those pupils of yours.

I still wake, eyes primed
irises retracted against the dark
like looking for a lover
who disappeared
in the night.

There

A young girl in labor
assigned to a know-nothing first year
who knew nothing but to wipe the sweat
from her forehead and pant along
as that mysterious animus deep within

roiled and twisted towards the surface
a creature from her very depths
every five minutes
then four. . . .
But I wasn't there.

And I wasn't there when she said
"something came out of me"
and the sheets flung themselves back
and a blue tentacle pulsed
between her legs

a terrifying reveal
but I wasn't there.
It was scarcely my gloved hand
that reached deep inside its lair
pushing the soft carapace

up, up—
back, back—
not yet, not now a faraway voice yells
pushing against nature pushing the gurney
into the hall seeking

the room where the giant light
illuminates like the sun above the ocean
prolapsed cord a voice cries *help*
now it's coming now and I don't know
how to make it stop.

The Breast Exam

I don't want to be the one to tell you
   your arms raised above your head
      as if in surrender

I don't want to be the one who says
   don't give up
      knowing you will be lucky to live

with pieces cut away
   I don't want to be the one anymore.
      I want to padlock the office

drop my cell phone in the dumpster
   lose myself in desire
      place my skin against my love's

allow my hands to caress
   and no longer examine
      I want to feel without worrying

what there is to feel
   I want to be the one
      to surrender.

Low Water Crossing

It's just a low spot in the road
a momentary dip on the way to work.
As days turned to decades
I've been through it all right here.

I have glimpsed spring's fleeting green
in shallow pools left in the wake of a shower.
Once a torrent almost washed me away
but I stopped and it all flowed by.

Wildflowers, gully glitter, disappeared
in the beat of a hummingbird's wing, always
before I thought to pick them.
Then the interminable heat. I am stifled

and grow brittle as the brown stalks
which line the way in summer. Dust devils
have sucked me dry.
All these years and still I lack the skin

of the prickly pear. Still lack the thorns.
I wait to be blown by the fronts of winter
tumbling along this shallow trough
to some final place, seeds all scattered.

But this morning, this brisk fall morning
when I should have worn a sweater
but didn't—after a cold rain onto a yet
warm earth—thick fog rose here

apparitions in quiet dampened places.
The gully smoldered serpentine in mist
and I stopped to breathe the musky smoke.
There's fire here. I know there's still fire.

This Sadness

is a cancer
    for which there is no cure
        a surgeon might

cut it out from its roots
    but it would grow back
        an obstetrician might attempt

a high forceps delivery
    a psychiatrist might try to talk it out
        but this sadness

        does not speak the language.

To the Medical Student Who Jumped
From the Roof of the Hospital

I know that place well
watched too many
sunsets in between
the despair of learning it all:
the bony articulations
the long path
the blood takes
to make its way
all the way down.
The sky was brilliant then
cascades of pink and red
where else could one view
such a spectacle?
The iron bars on the roof
were to keep the psychos
from heaving themselves off—
who else would do such a thing?
First do no harm, Hippocrates said
and I tried until
the nights on the wards
merged into the next day and the next
I watched the lights of the city ignite
then fade until the sky
bled morning
Once I thought I knew it all
an arrogance that soaks
into the skin like formaldehyde
for at the bedside in the end
there is only one's self to blame
and Hippocrates looks away
when another pair of lids is closed
All those nights: I waited patiently
for the rising of the moon
the turning of the constellations
but they ran together like
the seasons, away like the years

and I must admit
I looked for ways
to scale those bars myself
though they were too formidable
and I finished rounds instead
round and round
and round always trying to grasp
a handhold on what I knew
what I didn't know, searching
tomes heavier than newborns
for answers I have yet to find
often found myself despised
for being on that pedestal
for not being God
while hating myself unless
I could always be right
and I never could
Like me you were never taught
those center-of-gravity lessons
and landed feet first
in the doctors' parking lot
splintering
your tibias, fibulas
ramming
your femurs through your pelvis
rending
your femoral arteries
slicing
your aorta
when you left the ward early
Hippocrates glared at the
crimson horizon
I stared down still awaiting
the dawn.

Happiness Is Genetic Too

She called tonight to get this off her chest
something she read in *Newsweek,* new data
just out preliminarily at best—

Hey, she said, this one fact may spur new ways
to look at an old problem—like your height:
I mean short people can't help it anyway

it's just in their genes, strange nucleotide
sequences keeping them from full flower;
well, actually that's hard to verify

they've sprouted as much as they're supposed to.
Besides, there's more than just being taller.
Don't you see: being happy is out of your control

for now, of course, but finding that bad seed
is the first step to finding a real cure.
Sure—remember all the gene disease

they've fixed, well, theoretically there are
a lot of them on the drawing board, you
know what I mean, so tell me do you dare

be happy about this—in some small way?

Out of Practice

The end will come in its time
   the doctor penned and I guess
      thirty years—

a long marriage—
   ought to be enough.
      Ten thousand entries

fevered calls in the night
   sirens, blaring lights
      question after question

where is the pain?
   what makes it better?
      Fear and antiseptic

always in our room—
   god I want to forget
      all that dis-ease

take back that news
   that terrible news
      the yellow suffering

of which we will die
   miserably
      and too soon

Oh how you embraced me
   your hand cool
      on my forehead

I recorded demise
   in a radiant scrawl
      but there were never

      enough flowers

Something must always wear out
and no one
can always be right—

Remember how we
loved each other once

I have done the best I could.

Non-Stop Flight

My grandmother could quiet this child—somehow she would:
some kind of tea, a soulful rocking, humming.
Once I had little girls of my own; even then
I was always the wrong kind of doctor.

I'm sorry, I tell the mother, *I guess I don't know much about*
babies anymore. Must be an ear infection or something.
We'll be on the ground soon.
She is relieved to have her baby handed back

even though the little girl is screaming as loud as before.
You did your best, she says.
I sit back down but leave my belt unbuckled; the baby's
cries pierce the cabin. I close my eyes, turn off

the reading light but I can't rest.
All I know is this: if this were my baby
if this were the middle of the night
I would call the pediatrician. I would go to the emergency room.

I would wait to be seen. I would hang on the doctor's words.
I would go to the all-night pharmacy. I would dribble
the medicine into her somehow. I would wait.
Lacking wisdom, I would wait.

Gardeners

You cannot justify a garden to nonbelievers.
—*Maxine Kumin in "Jicama, without Expectation," from*
Prairie Schooner, *Spring 1994*

Middle age and I'm turning my first garden:
soil desert-thin, rain so slight except when
it comes in torrents, runs off before
I know, nothing to hold it back, nothing in
abundance except the unforgiving sun.
I will never have a New England garden
a temperate Eden where another digger
started early: cleared and composted, mulched
and mulched—it is not possible to have
too much mulch she says—while hurrying
spring on south-facing sills. Then planted

and hoed, harvested and jarred and canned.
And what she has reaped: basil and eggplant,
cabbage, cauliflower and asparagus
in May; beets and peas, cucumbers and beans
and corn—that sweet Silver Queen in August—
strawberries, raspberries to jelly, to jam, to put up
and share; and into November beets and cukes
and brussels sprouts—and oh Sweet Mama—winter squash.
I will never have a harvest like hers: my roots
go mostly to tops; I will pluck a few
tomatoes, a small onion or two

perhaps a pepper if I get lucky; maybe
even a few forgotten leaves of lettuce
but never enough to toss a salad
of any succulent consequence.
Yet I will be content to turn
earth each fissured spring
and sow this patch of seed
then treat myself to whatever might
come up. And, yes: to keep on until
the heat burns what little remains
of my dry tangle to ash.

Common Texas Grasses—A Guide

—for Frank Gould, Professor of Range Science

April
and I wade in
the sea of grass around me
shoulder high, your book in my hand.
Recognition of grasses, you say, is based on color
the feel of the sod, the time of year it greens up,
the flowering tip, the basic unit.
The exact identity of a grass, you write

*can be determined on the basis
of just one tiny inflorescence.*
And I try, Frank, but I'm drowning
in green with my old eyes
and it's a spring day, your guide
my bible, so I sit in the grass
and the wind ripples my hair and the prairie,
my face in your book wishing you were here to help

I daydream of western wheatgrass and little bluestem
oldfield threeawn, sideoats grama, the downy brome
little quakinggrass, rabbitfootgrass, rescue grass
of fluffgrass, tall fescue, little barley and green sprangletop
the bush muhly, beaked panicum and longtom
of switchgrass, cupgrass, sixweeksgrass
the tall dropseed, needle and thread, crinkleawn
and tumble lovegrass and nimblewill

of maidencane and the weeping lovegrass
all waving in the wind on my piece of the prairie
then weeping for you, Frank
who spent a life writing it all down
an inflorescence of man
among the grasses
I hope you are at peace
under yours.

Shock and Awe in Comfort, Texas

This morning I walk to the pond
sit at the edge of the water
on the concrete stoop the German
homesteader built thick as a bunker
to reconnoiter his domain

out of nowhere dragonflies dive-bomb
their rivals and from the near bank
a frog screams, his leg in the grip
of a moccasin's jaw, screams
until he is swallowed whole

then phoebes join the fray and tear
the Red Admirals from mid-air
while a snapper sucks a duckling
down in one gasp
the Red-Shouldered hawk whirls

and shrieks in the field below
his laser eyes on the rabbit
that becomes his prize
while the black vultures
captivated by the scent

boil above a gut-shot antelope.
There will be no peace today
in Comfort, Texas
so I rise from my position
for the world to see

and a great blue heron
flaps away from the shore
the jays dash into the thickets
and I stride back to the house
leaving in the wake of my boots

not one blade of prairie grass
not one bluebonnet standing.

What I Remember of Embryology

Tethered
we are all waiting
fetuses suckling
our way

to heart and hair
teeth and bone
reaching grasping
limb buds into fingers

transforming
gill slits to lungs
eyespots
into eyes of blue

forever focusing
too much
on the next stage
that inevitable

recapitulation
please
just let me float
in the amnion

until it is my turn
to be born.

B-Ball Lament

Spring thaw
and I watch

two boys go
one–on–one

dribbling
faking

shooting almost
perfect parabolas

one bare-chested
muscled

the other rippling
under a tee shirt.

Once I was
just like them

but I haven't
played

in decades
gave up

ball-bouncing for
balancing

an act
requiring

no movement
and only

the shallowest
of inhalations

exhalations
yet today standing

in the sunlight
my hands yearn

to cradle the ball
my arms and shoulders

feel the rhythm
of its return

my legs and hips
want to pivot

on the asphalt
feint and roll

circle and jump
ball gently

leaving my fingertips
high arcing shot

only the coarse swish
of the net

to break
the downward slide.

What Mick's Got

—for B and S

He likes the mall his father tells me and I say fine
since I'm only back for a few hours anyway
and Mick just born the last time I saw him
now careens through the crowd
big smile on his face burbling to himself
his dad slithering through the Christmas crush to keep Mick in sight
and it's the food court first and Mick stays within reach as the burgers
are flamed by sour-faced teenagers—the look Mick's daddy and I had
when we first met many McPounds ago—and we follow Mick to his favorite
table but there's a woman at it and he stares at her for a few seconds
and she starts to smile but he's already turned on his heels at the sound of
his father's voice: *Let's try this one Mick*
and today it's okay and Mick sits quietly for a moment
between us studies his burger and fries chews on the straw in his Coke
Yeah my friend says *my parents and my six-year-old*
all of them in diapers
and Mick takes a piece of burger in his hand nibbles at it
chortles then his face lights up like a tree ornament and he's out of his seat
off across the courtyard *He's headed for the Disney Store* my friend says
Listen would you mind getting these trays? and he's off spotting Mick a few
yards and I get ketchup all over my hands and say shit
and think about my wife whom I've left
about our kids somewhere fallen between the split
and I'm puffing when I catch up and Mick's watching a Goofy clock
then he's a little hummingbird staring down the Cheshire Cat
then gazing at the Fantasia video
entranced by the stars and moons and planets embroidered
into the carpeting underfoot skipping this way and that big grin on his face
back and forth back and forth
His daddy mirrors his steps to keep an eye on him in case
he bolts for the door which he will
The Nature Company is next my friend tells me and then
It's been a rough couple of years. . . . I'm better now on meds
and I know about this
better living through chemistry I say and we both laugh
and Mick is staring at the Goofy clock again

I'd like to buy that for him I say and my friend says
He won't acknowledge it you know
I know about that I say as I take it off the shelf and realize that it runs
backwards the numbers flipped the second hand ticking off the years
counter-clockwise and I figure that's what's fascinating Mick and how it's
the kind of timepiece I could use myself and I pay for it
and Mick runs up to the cashier for a second
just as she looks at him he is away . . . *Cute kid* she says
then it's time for me to go and his daddy sweeps Mick up into his arms
and his son buries his face into his father's neck and says clear as day
Happy Happy Happy
He's a happy kid anyway my friend says to me
and I say he sure is then remembering it's time for my pill
time to jack up the level of something I must have in short supply
though now I know it will never be as good as what Mick's got.

On Slipping Through Terminal 1, Concourse C at O'Hare

First you descend, not all the way
but enough so jumbo jets can roll
across the tarmac caressing your hair while
music drifts—every song you
ever loved and then you are struck
by the lights, waves of neon rainbow rippling
racing overhead, drawing you onto
the moving path that carries you on more
quickly than you want to
go, pulling you through the dark tunnel
as the planes whine and rumble, readying
to spirit you away, tear you away
then far away at first her voice echoes
now clearly more clearly the siren calls:
please look down she whispers *the moving
sidewalk ends* she says *please look down* she sings
and you know what that means but you're gliding
way too fast yet still grounded and you gaze
up into the lilting luminescence
unconcerned about the fall.

The Teens
For Christ Convention
At the Holiday Inn

There were legions
of them.
There was just

the two of us.
They squeezed
their fervent bodies

into the elevators.
Our aging bones
rose up alone.

They frolicked
in the hall
stormed the Coke machine.

We closed the door
latched it
sipped wine

from plastic cups.
Revivaling
they whooped

they hollered
flush with body
and blood.

The spirit moved us.
They stayed awake
all hours

prayed for flesh
and absolution
left forlorn.

We made
hallowed sounds
left reborn.

Flu Season

It's nothing, you tell winter hordes
who break down the door
flooding the waiting room
with mucus, calling at all hours
it's nothing it's going to be
fine in a few days; go to bed
drink, take Tylenol by the clock
and you'll be fine in a few days
they listen, they trust
and you believe 'til after
the fiftieth, or maybe
the five hundredth case
The Crash—
the worst headache: maybe an
aneurysm leaking
The Chill—
virions rupturing
re-infecting, spilling
into blood, temperature spiking
like a patient in sepsis
like one with that virus
no one can cure
The Cough—
incessant, wracking
subduing, old man's friend
if only sleep would come
just go to sleep
but trachea on fire
bronchial tree burning
in spasms, animal feeding
on heart—maybe it's not
what you think—viral-ravaged
neurons conjuring every
disease you ever learned
ever dreaded
fever breaks, cleansing sweat
body still resolvable
slowly overcomes, antibodies
rescue this time
but you are not immune.

The Whistler

They come every four months
He smiles, drools, sits quietly
always says yes, only says yes

at her turn she bitches and sighs
bemoans and cries: *he's getting worse*
he's only getting worse

She can't take it anymore
and neither can I.
Have you considered a Home? I ask

my stethoscope on her chest
trying to discern
what's inside, looking into her

mascara-caked eyes now
red and ruined beyond relief
when she shyly says, *Doctor*

I've gotten so fat but do you know
he still whistles when
I take off my clothes

And he sits there smiling
smiling, grinning, nodding
Yes, he says. Yes.

What We Said

He said he was losing weight because his appetite was off, the stress and all that, but otherwise felt fine except for the heartburn that he'd always had, more or less, but she finally made him come in.

And I said how long have your eyes been this color and he shrugged and she said it's just the fluorescent lights and I said to him I think you should go into the hospital for some tests and he looked at me with those jaundiced eyes and asked: just for some tests? And I said yes.

There's a growth I said a day later as he lay in his yellowness on the starched white sheets. A growth he asked? That doesn't mean anything bad necessarily she said. Right, doctor? She looked at me her eyes brimming. I mean it could be a cyst, right? Just something filled with fluid? It could be, I said to him who didn't look back. A cyst she said.

The surgeon called me after the case and said what a mess it was in there but he thinks he got it all. You got it all? I asked. I think so he told me. But I'd have the oncologist see him anyway he said.

The surgeon thinks he got it all I said to the patient who was leaking out through his tubes. Thank God she said. Oh thank you doctor she said. We need to have an oncologist see him just in case I said.

In case? she said. Yes I said. As long as there's no chemotherapy she said. He doesn't want chemotherapy. I understand I said.

He was sitting up, the tubes were crawling out, the yellow waning when the nodes came back positive. He looks so good doctor, doesn't he look good? He could smile now that the stomach tube was out and he did. You're doing great I said. Listen, folks, some of the lymph nodes were positive . . .

Does that mean chemotherapy? she asked. He doesn't want chemotherapy she said. Let's have an oncologist see him first I said. That's a good idea she said looking at him who said nothing.

The oncologist told me he had an excellent chance of remission on the new multi-drug regimen. How long? I asked. Six months. A year maybe longer he said. How toxic? I asked. We can handle most of the side effects he said. And without treatment? I asked. You know he said.

The oncologist recommends chemotherapy I said to them. He was sitting in a chair a tray of food gone cold before him. He just won't eat doctor she said. We'll try liquid supplements I said. That's a good idea she said.

About the chemotherapy I said, it may kill any tumor cells that remain. But I thought the surgeon got it all? she said. When the lymph nodes are positive we can never be sure I said. He doesn't want chemotherapy she said. I looked at him. His eyes were clearer now.

Here is what I wanted to say: Go home. Get out of this place. Eat chocolate and pizza, ice cream and french fries when you can, go fishing, take a trip around the world, tell your kids you love them, read mystery novels, go to the movies, watch the clouds drift by, write your memoir, make love to your wife. But go just go.

I guess I should fight this thing right doc? he said.

You should I said.

Triage

Tell me, what is it you plan to do with your one wild and precious life?
—Mary Oliver in "The Summer Day," from New and Selected
Poems, *Beacon Press, 1992*

I never cared who made the world:
the swan, the black bear, the grasshopper
I used myself up worrying over

the obsolescing parts—splinting
the wing, bandaging the paw, aligning
the mandible. I washed

thousands of times between
procedures, barely noticed that the mended
rose again from the table

while I went on to the next broken piece.
Until it was me who needed fixing
but where I looked I found only

complicated eyes
until I ran wild
into the unplowed fields

until the only arms
around me
were my own.

Letting It Go

—for Dr. S.

Tied into that chair
he's come
full circle
sits outside
the nurses station

watching his world
in shift rotations
likeable old gent
but he can't hear
our exhortations

it's that smile
he gets just before
he lets it go
part relief part
wicked anticipation

the nurses know
ask me year
after year in consternation
*Can't we just put
in a catheter?*

and I always say *No!*
without hesitation
lecture on infections
then pat him on the shoulder
as if to say: *Well done!*

And one day
when I lie in my own pool
of self-reflection
I will savor
that warmth tickling

the remains of my erection
patiently await
their arid ministrations
and with that my own
powdery resurrection.

A Sigh on Rounds

White coat, rubber gloves
my instrument dangling

but she finally died
after such a struggle—the young

always struggle so—
I listened to her chest

till it stopped then clicked
off the machine.

It sighed for us all as the air
drained out. And the moon

was still low in the sky
so large, so round—this

is a shape I know well—
and it hung there like a silver disc

auscultating the earth
But I could no longer listen

as I sat on a night lawn
slowly moistening.

Discharges

Soundproof cubicle: me and the dictaphone
a pile of charts, ghosts of patients past
I remember that night I admitted her
so short of breath her only voice

muffled in exhalations
and him—arteries corroded
like pipes in high-rise slums—
organs toppling, slammed

by wrecker balls: heart, brain, kidneys
finally that gangrenous leg—I had signed
everything but the DNR order
and now it stares at me again months

after they laid him in the ground.
Those medical record clerks
stalk until every command is confirmed.
I top off the mound, linger a moment

still stunned and they assault me
suddenly with more charts slammed
onto the desk like discharges
in urban canyons, screams

that echo long after the admissions
have died away.

Sherbet

A few weeks after her discharge
after the legions of modern miracles
met her dauntless infirmity
I finally retreated.

She waits now
in this way station
where I come
no longer in white.

And she is weary
a shadow
staring out the window
the tray of clotted

food nearby
and I ask how she feels
but she does not answer.
The raspberry sherbet is melting

yet it is the only treatment
a plastic spoon my only instrument
and I bring it to her parched lips
and she eats for me.

I say isn't the sky so blue
today the clouds so white
spring is near I say
all the time feeding her

urging her to take every drop.
But I am not used
to this work and a dollop
drops on her gown

and red spreads across her chest.
I swipe it away with my hand.
I'm sorry I say
I'm so sorry.

Clinic

When will my eyes
be as vacant as his

my pulse as weak
my joints as stiff

when will I need
my first walker

first wheelchair
has the cell

that is parent
to my cancer

already mutated
are there now two

four, eight, sixty-four
have they broken

ten thousand
when will my heart

beat in that erratic
way, require a jump-start

when will it—once
and for all—stop

when will my skin take
on that look

in certain light
it has already

when will I forget
your name

my own?

Side Show

Come one come all see what awaits you
amazing death-defying acts by
octogenarians
and even older
the barker in white coat stands center
station flipping his instrument
see the Pretzled Woman
living on green drool
grass-snaked through her nose all
the way to her gullet and over here we have
Vacant Man—watch his chest
rise and fall
in perfect
syncopation with the mechanical
sighs of loved ones who said
do everything you can . . .
you be the judge
then thrill as poisons
pummel Mister Neoplasia
a race to the finish
see what's eating
his hairless hopeless carcass
then gasp at
grandma's wire act
heart stopping spells
of fatal fibrillation deftly
thwarted by a thin strand
threaded through
amazed arteries
into a heartsick ventricle
shocked and dazzled by joules
pulsed along its length
death defying death denying
how long can this go on?

Step right up—don't be the last in line.

Hometown Girl

—for Dorothy B.

The first time we met you called me "hon"
in that voice I knew right away was born
on the shores of the Chesapeake
where I was raised so long ago.
And you even longer.
Here we are in the photo your daughter
snapped in the hospital room: me
in my starched coat, stethoscope dangling
across my tie, leaning in next to your bed
you with the oxygen in your nose reclining
white hair all primped. I helped you get ready.

We both tried to smile; you still had your jowls.
I want to forget all that disease
I treated you for: the kidney we plucked,
the aorta we patched, the emphysema
we placated, the pneumonias, the collapsed
vertebrae, the cancer in the end. God, I want
to forget that. I want to forget all
the pills I prescribed and you swallowed,
all the treatments. I want to give you back
all the blood we drew from your withdrawing
veins. I want to take back all the bad news

I ever had to give.
I want to remember those years
when you were spiffy. When you came
to the office in flowery blouses, pantsuits
gold jewelry and pearls.
I want to remember your voice, that gravelly
twang from our old hometown. I want us
to talk about Charles Street, Hutzlers,
the Orioles at the old ballpark, the Bay,
rockfish, and crackin' steamed crabs.
I miss you hon.

Image courtesy of Jeffrey M. Levine

Raising Money for Medical Bills

Can you not see her there
swaddled in white
hidden behind her cataract veil?

On your clenched fist
is a golden ring so surely you
remember that day

so expectant now so faraway . . .
The sounds of her tiny organ
drifting up from the street

echoing something you
heard once from the loft
of a church

or perhaps in an elevator.
You carry a black bag now
always rushing

your own white garment shed long ago
but don't you see she needs more
than care dispensed with a pen.

She's begging you now
to stop . . . listen, listen
and look into her face.

Can't you see the angels
trailing behind her?
Benevolent attendants who

will escort you one day
to that white world you conceive.
Or not.

The Tyranny of Aging

She'll soon be ninety-five, struggling to stay alive
after that last stroke left one-half paralyzed.
More encouragement is what she needs
I tell her worried old son as I leave

the daily, shift by shift progress of this
tortured recuperative process:
the fatigue, the frailty, the torn rice paper skin
the thick syllables, the bottom reddening.
Yet she understands every word, tries, tries
puts up with our constant entreaties:
Yes, that's it, that's it we say, *see there's movement
coming back, keep pushing, work every moment,
you don't live to be your age by giving up.*

Wake up, pull up, sit up, cough that junk up
And, you know, she's improving: the feeding
tube is out, she's talking more, drinking
Ensure, the therapist has her bearing weight
on the good leg. I'm planning a discharge date
okay, to a nursing home, but a good one.
She'll have visitors—her "boy"—flowers, the sun.
*She just needs to keep up the hard work
push a little more* say the aides and clerks

Now today I'm in the stairwell hushed, head spinning
heart pounding, mind-weary from all this rounding
I have to go to her now—doctor-calm, manner mild—
to say I just closed the lids on her last living child.

Redbud

March—I walk
the ravines, the treed
windbreaks, the creek bottom
all the wooded places

searching for redbuds.
One hundred acres and you
are the only one I have ever found
and I never know

waiting through each winter
if you have survived—
your spindly trunk
born from the side of a dead oak

and year after year
you bend more and more
toward the light which filters
through the canopy

of hackberry and cedar.
In one night a winter-hungry deer
might strip your bark
down through the cambium

and you'd be gone.
But this morning here you are
your blossoms fragile, so few
the color so faint it's fanciful

to call it red.
Here you are
and here I am
hanging on.

Blue Period

He hangs the paintings himself
centers the homemade frames

tacks the nails into the sheetrock.
They hang like the second-hand suits

and pants, jackets and overcoats
the instruments and cheap luggage

all the *objets d'art* in that
hand-me-down shop where he spent

himself for so many years.
The colors of his palette:

steel blue, ocean blue, storm blue
lost horizon blue. In his paintings

blue vases cradle blue asters
delphiniums, lilacs, hydrangeas

irises. The canvases drip
blue into my rooms, my eyes

my father's blue.
His clothes hang on him now

he is gaunt as the man
with the blue guitar.

Vermilion eludes him
stains the walls I try to breach—

blue light for the son
who still waits for the blood

to come back
in his father's face.

Moon Over Twin Sisters Peak

—for Michael Jay, my brother

Do you remember that night?
The harvest moon astride the two hills
like the world on the shoulders of Atlas.

It took my breath away as we
crested the rise and I braked hard
swung the truck off the road

scattering gravel
into the undercarriage.
You had come out to the country that day

and we walked back to the lake
threw some lures at the fish
like we did when we were kids.

The week before
our father
asked me who I was.

They named those peaks for two sisters
their parents killed by Kiowas
a century and a half ago.

How those girls must have wailed
and held fast to one another then.
It was time to head back to the city

but we sat in silence and let the sounds
of the Texas night fill the cab and watched
the moon rise as if it weighed nothing

watched as it receded
until it was only a thin disc high in the sky
just a small glimmering thing.

And you said, *That's something, isn't it?*
I nodded in the dark, turned the key
slipped a CD into the player

Willie Nelson crooning *Stardust*
a song our father used to whistle
and we headed back to town.

Dragonfly

When dragonfly enthusiasts meet over beer, the talk invariably turns
to how some prized specimen has eluded them and to new schemes for
evening the odds.
　　—Smithsonian, *July 1996*

Ornament of summer, odd combination of beautiful things
did you not know your metamorphosis was incomplete?
Oh, Green Darner, Gilded River Cruiser, Calico Pennant

servant of snakes they called you, devil's darning
needle stitching the lips of wicked children while they sleep
eye sticker, mule killer—it's a wonder you survive

these years living on the run: voracious nymph
gobbling mosquito wigglers with your adolescent lips, even
froglets if they get too close, and suddenly you emerge

without a rest, take a breath, split your skin, stretch
wings and abdomen, triple your size in no time
Oh, Beaverpond Baskettail, Meadowhawk, Sandhill Bluet

you who outmaneuver all other winged insects, you, chitinous
master of unstable aerodynamics with the Cyclops eye
misty and deep like the fortune-teller's ball, now they know

your deadly looking tail has no sting, that the worst
you can inflict is a good pinch, that you carry
no disease, damage no crop, that there are others

of you to find, to name, to dip into acetone
and slide into glassine envelopes. Now they
know your secret: that first you

have sex with yourself, anoint
your body's distant tip with sperm
before you embrace your love, hold

her against you, undulate in space, all the while reaching
inside of the one now in your grasp, scraping out the unseen
seed of your rival, so she will, in the end, hold only your own.

There is no rest for you: no cocoon, no chrysalis
now you must defend a perch, a lone reedy site
against relentless competition—and you fly, you buzz

in tandem with him, guard him, cling to him
eliminate him from the copulatory race, though he
is no longer the enemy. Beware. Primitive legions covet

your odd modernity, hunt you down with water guns
and nets: *Anax junius, Epitheca princeps, Calopteryx maculata.*
oh, Lord and Master of June; oh, Prince; oh, Jewelwing.

Mowing

My father, a renter of rowboats
pushed a hand mower back and forth
across our yard and I groaned
when he called me for a turn
though it must have made him strong
since he lived long enough
to forget his name
and then my own.
I was the success he was not
and now I've got too much to mow
even if I had the will to push
I no longer have the strength
so I bought a tractor to cruise
this lush prairie, an inland sea
the blades whir like great propellers
as I sit astride the craft
watch the blue eyes roll
from the blue-eyed grass
the seed heads tumble
from the turgid thistle dropping
into the waving stands of three-awn
while the breaching grama is sliced clean
across my now shorn refuge
and the blades whirl beneath me
the engine moans
shivering in my bones—those
rotating sabers turning grinding
lull me from all memory
and only the crack
of something unexpected
recaps the carnage to come.
Where is the Captain now?
I know there are shoals but
I am mowing I am mowing
and only the shallows remain.
Father, see my wake
how straight and neat the rows.

Red Oak

You know the one we pass
on the plateau when we walk
back to the lake together
your hand in mine

though not often these days
my daughter, now
that you are grown, married.
The seasons shift subtly here

but this tree never forgets the fall
its leaves turning scarlet
with the first hard push of cold
then dropping

one by one and then in a torrent
until it is bare for the winter.
But not barren—never
barren. Remember this.

Especially this morning after your loss
after you hang up the phone and cry
again some more. There is green
just waiting to surge

the sap
just waiting to rise.

Free Range

It looks like rain this morning
when I go out into the fields
but of course here in July
it doesn't rain.

I go out hoping for a downpour
feel the dry weeds
the horehound, the coneflowers
crunch under my feet

walk across great patches
of cracked earth where
harvester ants plow
their circles of bare ground

their meticulous routes running
north south, east west.
Only the grasshoppers seem alive
thousands fly like sparks off the toes

of my boots as I walk to the barn.
Nothing eats what you got here
the county agent said, *that's why
it's still here.*

And I think about those old Germans
scratching a living off this place, sucked
dry by skies like these, promising clouds
and the smell of rain that never falls

but every few years when it comes heavy
in the winter and the Indian grass and bluestem
the switchgrass and sideoats grama
turn that hopeful green in the spring

in a year like that—like this—
the grasshoppers flare up
a wildfire out of nowhere
gnawing at every last green shoot

every juicy blade that maybe
with a little luck a little more rain
might have become milk or beef.
Now I'm at the barn, at the coop

where the Leghorns and Barred Rocks
squawk, line up at the gate
long for me to let them out
to let them eat their fill.

Feeding the Fish

Sometimes I walk to the lake
to feed the fish on a calm day
the ripples quelled
early morning, the light
slanting in just so

and then I see them
rising from the weedbeds
taking the little pellets of food
I throw in one handful after another.
Only the bluegills come darting

dainty little creatures—striped blue bodies
orange and red opercula.
In the dappled light they look
dressed for a fiesta
circling through the best part

of their day like dancers
sashaying up and back
in the sunlight waiting
for the feed to drift
down through the water

like manna from heaven.
While the bass silently
wait like submarines
deep and out of the morning light
wait until I am distracted

by the wingbeats of the killdeer
as he wheels in for a landing
sees me sitting on a rock
poised—my glasses
up to my face as if

ready to give some command—
before he flies off
with a sharp cry.
Then suddenly I hear
that sucking sound

turn back to see the circle
of lake pulled into
a vortex from the deep.
Sometimes I think the world
will end like this.

Plastic Caskets

Anticipating the boom in the demise of Boomers
they're fashioning terminal boxes out of space-age
material selling them mail-order through Amazon.
The same stuff as your hula hoop and Tonka toys
like the bumpers on your BMW like the tiles
on the Shuttle for God's sake.

Doesn't this give you a sense of security?
Think how long they will last—would you want anything less
after all that cholesterol counted those fat calories denied
miles jogged or cycled or rowed right there in your living room
groovin' on *Saturday Night Live*? Think of it:
impermeable to the damp the cold the worms

you lying there in your Gore-Tex shroud
atop the optional Thinsulate-lined silicone-filled simulated water bed
Awaiting the reassuring snap like the cap of your Mont Blanc
or that case which once cradled your birth control pills.
Hermetically sealing O-rings screen out what you've been
trying to avoid anyway these fleeting above-ground years.

Then on the CD clicks: all your digitized jpegged prerecorded
favorites—Bread Cream Meatloaf—infinite
soul-sustenance rocking on nuclear-powered batteries
half-lives measured in many multiples of that older model
you have finally upgraded.
And the quartz clock with its super triple-twist LED

above your eyes pulses to life
begins the long countdown.

Goshawk

—for RLM

It is not yet spring. The tree above your grave
is still barren of leaves, so it is easy
to see him swoop into the branches, swept-back
wings, white slash above his eyes, fleeing

winter, excited I guess by the flash
of forsythia, or those daffodil shoots
pushing up firm as we used to be
teenaged boys, adolescent travelers, you watched

birds with me, fixed them in your mind while I
fumbled with the field guide—*who cares what they're called,*
you said, *just watch now . . . look!*
I don't need a guide any longer at least

for the ones I find in our old neighborhood,
the ones I have seen time and time again
since you are gone, since you were laid to rest
the footstone says April 15, 1980

both of us thirty-two then and I keep coming
back year after year, and it is never quite spring here.
The goshawk watches me place a stone on your grave.
Until the warblers and the tanagers return

until the vireos and grosbeaks, the flycatchers
and orioles brave their one-night star-led flight
across the Gulf to make their way back dodging
utility wires and planes and high-rises

reflective glass mimicking open sky
and the cold if it's too early, the cold.
Until they return, the hawk bides his time watches me
snatches sparrows and mourning doves those others

too timid to make the fall trek to the Yucatan
or Costa Rica or Colombia.
He is biding his time watching me put stones
on your grave and I can almost hear you ask if maybe

I don't have something better to do, but it's not yet
spring—those barren trees—and I think there's plenty
of time. Then suddenly wonder why your mother
who still tints her hair blue at the beauty shop every week

who still has your thin and wrinkle-free face has already
set her footstone next to yours, waiting.
A grieving mother it reads, the date of her death—
like mine—not yet chiseled in stone.

And the goshawk screams and wheels through the treetops
circles and banks: *cree cree* he cries, warning how swift
he travels, how impatient for spring and other
fancies. And now so am I, sun on me, buds

burst and my jacket is off and I sit on your stone
sense you in the grass on the wind.
Old friend I will not be here early again.
Spring is for flight and mass migrations, it is

for spying chachalacas in the underbrush
scarlet macaws and golden-headed quetzals in lush
rain forest canopies where I will need the complete guide.
Look for me in winter white very late.

Perseids

have been forever
glancing
off the earth
August nights
unbeknownst to me

a few random
streaks per hour
slice the night sky
best viewed
under a moon

subdued
but who has the time
as the constellations rise
and fall
the Milky Way

turns and glows
but tonight I lingered
long enough to watch
two lines of light emerge
from a distant

radiant of sky
flare and intersect
burn for a moment
longer than a moment
brilliant enough

that I crave more
and wish I'd gone
gazing
last night as well
and all the nights before.

Dark Side

Once we were flower children
bathed in the numinous

now but daisies plucked and plucked
beneath a pocked chunk

of airless earth
only the dark side

exposed as you circle
endlessly

I dream now of that other side
of blood on the sheets

and those fragments of innocence
carried home with such care

forget the cosmic dust
with its footprints of strangers

by now you must have age spots
on your arms

old love—show me your face
your true face.

A Paper Anniversary at 52

—for Lee

And now you sleep in the bed left over
from your first marriage, tucked
into the only room of this old farmhouse
that's warm when the wind comes
from the north.
These walls are paper thin and mice live
within them and bigger things in the attic
where I have yet to go.
There are children of ours somewhere in the world
older than we were at our first unions.
The lake is almost dry from the drought
and the old garden is nothing but weeds
and the rock walls are falling down
and the barn is red from rust more than paint.
And we gave it all up for this:
that bluebirds will find the box you helped me
nail to the fencepost across the field from
the kitchen window;
that the martins will nest in the house atop
the pole you held as I hoisted all the way up;
that the thistles will be fewer next spring
now that we have wrestled so many out of the ground;
that another year like another season
will never be enough
until it is over.

Blue Norther

The norther blows in like a freight train
roaring around the house whistling
through the bare branches of the pecans
a two-comforter night you and me huddled
until morning breaks and the mist rises
off the creek beyond the bedroom window

and the mugs of coffee I make warm our hands
enough to get us layered up for our walk
back to the lake because I know they will be there
and we can see our breath in the air and steam
rises off the water now that the wind has settled
and we crouch in the switchgrass which has died back

again this winter and crawl on our knees
our bones aching from the cold and I help you
up the side of the berm which holds back the water
shushing you kicking aside
the empty shells of turtles bleached
by last summer's sun and we keep together

your hand in mine until we crest
the ridge and I pass you the glasses
I know they will be here swooping in
with the wind like they do year after year
and they are—rafts of them
shovelers and wigeons and scaups and ring-necks

bobbing in the mist staying close for warmth
and protection and you look
and let out a small gasp to see them so close
the green sheen of their heads the jet-black shine
off their backs the proud way they hold themselves
once again in breeding plumage

and we are both so cold trying to stay hushed
each in our own thoughts
remembering lives before the other
but then one of us—it was me—shifts
his bones and rises just an instant
and then they rise

at once and with a sound like nothing
I've ever heard—a slurry of ducks and water
a rising whistling rush a roaring
like the push of time itself
that has brought all of us
here this morning.

The Day It Came In

I think I know how they felt
those dirt-poor folks in East Texas
on the day that first wellhead blew
and thick gushes of Black Gold spewed out

like there was no tomorrow
and they thought it would never end
just get up in the morning collect you
a few barrels on your way to town

on the way to the bank on your way
to everything you ever wanted in your life
anything you could ask for or dream of
until it quit coming out under its own

head but there was still plenty
you just had to suck on the ground a little
like Yoo-Hoo through a straw but it was
still sweet crude and plentiful

and the accounts overflowed but
then it wasn't too long and you had to start
drilling deeper sucking harder
but you still had plenty in reserves they said

so no one really worried until a well
here and there went dry
and you started trying things like
injecting steam under pressure

to loosen the really pithy stuff
you knew was down there
if you could just get to it
But in the meantime the bills

came rolling in, the wife left
and you had to hock your Rolex
sell one of your Caddies
urge your daughter

to marry someone in high tech
all the time figuring that
maybe if you sank a hole
in some unexplored corner

of the old place you might hit
another gusher—that Black Gold
shooting again into the sky
better than any rainbow.

Overwinter

It was the winter of the ladybug invasion—
intractable cold, the woodstove burning oak
by the cord and they came in through every crack
looking to overwinter
not even to make babies, just to keep from freezing.
The walls, the ceilings crawled with them

and we tried gently picking each one, carrying him
or her to the door but more came in
so it was a losing proposition.
We decided to leave them be
and wait for spring when they
might find their way out on their own

though neighbors complained
of the yellow stains they left on furniture
but *who cares* we said
we are all yellow stains eventually.
Then there was that night—after a slight warming—
that it started to rain and lightning stabbed

the bedroom and thunder buffeted the house
and the knotty pine ceiling over our bed
shone with ladybug carapaces
each a smooth coppery nail head
and as the storm moved closer the thunder echoed
in the limestone canyon where the creek ran strong

just below, thunder enough
so the ladybugs showered down upon us
and we hunkered under the quilt
we'd bought at a garage sale and I must have fallen
asleep, you curled up into me, because I heard someone
far away—then close—call that it was time to go

someone called and I answered loudly in my sleep
I'm not ready but I
wasn't sure anymore if maybe it was time after all—
but you awakened, then woke me
brought me cold spring water to drink
and in your arms the season changed

Auscultation

Beyond the stacks
of textbooks studied

among the piles of journals
read and not

pulsing in
glove-numbed hands

inside the stiff white coat
starched to armor

noosed in the caduceus
drumming deep within

the black coils

between the endless rounds
the endless dyings

still beats
a poet's heart

and it pounds again
and pounds again

now that I
clutch

this instrument
to my own chest.

Acknowledgments and Permissions

Acknowledgments

I am indebted to the entire staff at Kent State University Press for their help and professionalism in bringing this book into the world—with a special "thank-you" to Joyce Harrison, the original Acquiring Editor, who saw promise in my words.

I wish to thank Alan Shapiro for his encouragement of my work twenty years ago while I was his student at the Bread Loaf Writers' Conference, as well as his kindness in agreeing to write the foreword to this book. Maxine Kumin was also a source of advice and wisdom as a writing mentor and a friend during the last decades of her life. Edward Hirsch and Phil Levine were patient and inspiring teachers.

Professor Mike Rosenzweig nurtured my interest in ecology, evolution, and the natural world when I was his undergraduate student at Bucknell University. His teachings, research, and friendship have enriched my life, and the lives of his many other students.

I am indebted to my friend and fellow geriatrician, Dr. Jeffrey Levine, an accomplished artist and photographer, who has graciously allowed me to use two of his photographs for this book. His work brings realism, compassion, and poignancy that honors the elderly all over the world.

I have a special appreciation for Dr. Michael A. LaCombe, the poetry editor for the *Annals of Internal Medicine*. His thirty years of dedication to and advocacy for physician writers has been extraordinary. Thanks to him—and a few others—many wonderful doctor-poets have emerged from the shadows and into the mainstream of the medical humanities renaissance.

There are others to thank: Karen Subach at the Iowa Writers' Workshop; Wendy Barker and Catherine Kasper at The University of Texas at San Antonio; Nan Cuba and Sheila Black at Gemini Ink; and Barbara Ras at Trinity University Press.

In addition, I want to thank former and current colleagues at The Center for Medical Humanities and Ethics at the University of Texas Health Science Center at San Antonio these last fifteen years: Marvin Forland, Ruth Berggren, Richard Usatine, Jason Morrow, Abraham Verghese, Tess Jones, and Craig Klugman.

I also want to thank my mother, Francis Winakur, who raised me with high expectations. I have tried to live up to them. At 93, she keeps my geriatric skills honed. She is always a source of inspiration for my writings. As is my love for my brother, Michael.

My daughters, Betsy and Emily, are both accomplished writers, teachers, and critics. Their comments on early versions of many of these poems only helped make them better. Their support and love of their father only made me a better person. May they, one day, read these poems to their children—Jonah, Sophie, and Ella—so they may better know and remember their grandfather.

Finally, my wife, Lee Robinson, an accomplished writer and poet, provided encouragement and wise critique for which I can never begin to adequately thank or repay. It is her love and understanding that I can only do my best to return in kind.

Permissions

"Ascultation" and "Sherbet" were first published in 2005 in *Annals of Internal Medicine,* 142(11): 951 and 142(4): 301, respectively.

"Ascultation" and "The Whistler" from *Body Language: Poems of the Medical Training Experience* edited by Neeta Jain, Dagan Coppock, and Stephanie Brown Clark. Copyright © 2006 by Jerald Winakur. Used with the permission of The Permissions Company, Inc., on behalf of BOA Editions, Ltd., www.boaeditions.org.

"Clinic" was originally published in *On Being a Doctor 3: Voices of Physicians and Patients,* edited by Christine Laine and Michael A. LaCombe (American College of Physicians, 2007) and appears courtesy of the American College of Physicians.

"Rounds" was originally published in *Journal of General Internal Medicine* 22.11 (January 2007): 1624. Copyright © 2007, Society of General Internal Medicine. Reproduced with permission of Springer.

"A Paper Anniversary at 52" was originally published in *Poetry* 181.4 (February 2003): 258.

"To the Medical Student Who Jumped from the Roof of the Hospital" was originally published in *The New Physician* 48:7 (October 1999): 9–10.

"A Sigh on Rounds" was originally published in *Pulse* (February 2015).

"Moon Over Twin Sisters Peak" was originally published in the *San Antonio Express-News* on June 7, 2009, and appears courtesy of the *San Antonio Express-News.*

"Gardeners" was originally published in *The Quiet Born from Talk,* edited by Catherine Kasper (Creative Writing Program–UT San Antonio, 2015).

These four poems were originally published in the *Cumberland Poetry Review:* "Are Butterflies Birds?" (Fall 1995), "A Denunciation of Quarks" (Fall 1995), "Dragonfly" (Fall 1997), and "The Teens for Christ Convention at the Holiday Inn" (Fall 1997).

These three poems were originally published in *Mediphors: A Literary Journal of the Health Professions:* "The Breast Exam" (as "Surrender") and "This Sadness," Spring/Summer 1996, and "The Whistler" (as "He Still Whistles"), Fall 1996.

LITERATURE AND MEDICINE

Michael Blackie, Editor • Carol Donley and Martin Kohn, Founding Editors